SOME RAIN

James Edward Luczak

BROADWAY PLAY PUBLISHING INC
224 E 62nd St, NY, NY 10065
www.broadwayplaypub.com
info@broadwayplaypub.com

SOME RAIN
© Copyright 1982 James Edward Luczak

All rights reserved. This work is fully protected under the copyright laws of the United States of America. No part of this publication may be photocopied, reproduced, stored in a retrieval system, or transmitted, in any form or by any means, electronic, mechanical, recording, or otherwise, without the prior permission of the publisher. Additional copies of this play are available from the publisher.

Written permission is required for live performance of any sort. This includes readings, cuttings, scenes, and excerpts. For amateur and stock performances, please contact Broadway Play Publishing Inc. For all other rights please contact B P P I as well.

Cover art by Craig Nealy

First edition: January 1983
This edition: May 2017
I S B N: 978-0-88145-001-9

Book design: Marie Donovan
Play text set in Baskerville by BakerSmith Type, N Y C
Printed and bound in the U S A

CAST OF CHARACTERS

SERA. An aging waitress.

WALLY. A young hitch-hiker.

EDDIE. Owner of Eddie's Diner. Sera's employer of 25 years.

SYNOPSIS OF SCENES

ACT I, SCENE 1

Trailer and yard. Around 6 in the p.m.

ACT I, SCENE 2

The same, about 1 hour later.

ACT II, SCENE 1

The same, but with the interior of trailer revealed. Some two hours later.

ACT II, SCENE 2

The same, early the next morning.

SET

To one side a small, very old trailer resting on rotting wooden blocks. Near the door of the trailer, a small garden of dead flowers and dying weeds. Remaining area a junkyard of discardables: Rusted tin cans, rotted and rotting scraps of wood, a treadless tire torn and twisted, various lengths of rusted pipes, empty and near empty cans of paint, two small wooden barrels filled with rusted nails, an oil barrel black painted and partially rusted, an old rust stained bathroom sink, etc.

The ground, itself, is red/orange in color with patches of sun browned, dying grass. Vaguely discernable surrounding the yard and trailer are pine trees.

LION THEATRE

RED OAK PRODUCTIONS

presents

SOME RAIN

by

JAMES EDWARD LUCZAK

Directed by
DALE ROSE

Starring (in alphabetical order)

BLANCHE CHOLET **DAVID DAWSON** **LOREN HAYNES**

Set Design
JAMES WOLK

Costume Design
COLLEEN MUSCHA

Lighting Design
CANDICE DUNN

SOME RAIN was initially given a staged reading at the Eugene O'Neill Theater Center's National Playwrights Conference

CAST

(in order of appearance)

Sara .... BLANCHE CHOLET

Wally .... LOREN HAYNES

Eddie .... DAVID DAWSON

The action takes place in a trailer and yard in rural Alabama, late summer, 1968.

ACT I

Scene 1 — Early evening

Scene 2 — About an hour later

ACT II

Scene 1 — Two hours later

Scene 2 — Early the next morning

THERE WILL BE ONE TEN-MINUTE INTERMISSION

ACT 1

Enter SERA followed a few steps behind by WALLY. SERA is wearing a worn and dirty waitress uniform. WALLY is in faded, dirty dungarees and sweat drenched t-shirt. SERA is bearing upon her stooped shoulders and bowed head a fatigue that has been for many years constant and unrelenting. WALLY is carrying a small, stained and battered suitcase kept from falling completely apart by many knotted bits of string.

SERA is old in her 40's. She exudes tiredness. One cannot tell whether she was once pretty or even if she was ever young. She wears no make-up and her thick red hair flecked with grey is piled on top of her head with many ill-arranged pins and consequent loose ends. The tops of her stockings are wadded around her garters just above her knees. The stockings, themselves, are loose, twisted and have numerous runs.

WALLY is still young in his early 30's. There is a boyish handsomeness, a charming child-likeness about him. His dark hair is curly and disheveled, his skin bronzed, and his muscles developed. A desire to get somewhere coupled with a fear of settling down has kept him on the road since his early teens.

The sun, though setting, is still suffocatingly present. The temperature is 98 and the humidity factor 100. There is little shade and even less of a breeze. The sky is a glazed sheet of fire.

As WALLY enters he does so stumblingly for he is entangled up to his knees in sticka bushes. He beats at the thorny growth trying to break free of its hold. He oouches and ouches as the sticka bush fights back, pricking his fingers with its protective thorns.

WALLY: Goddamn! What is this place? The sticka bush capitol of the world? We gotta few of 'em 'round where I grow'd up, but they know their place. 'Round here they think they own the goddamn road.

SERA: 'Round here they do.

WALLY: And what am I supposed to do about that? Step outta their way?

SERA: If you don't want 'em stickin' all over you, yeah.

WALLY: *(To sticka bush as he beats at it with his suitcase.)* Get off me, will ya? What I look like a tree or somethin' you gotta come crawlin' all over me?

SERA: All you gotta do is watch where you walkin'.

WALLY: I been watchin', but it don't do no good. They still come after me.

SERA: If you don't bother them they don't bother you.

WALLY: I gotta right to be walkin' where I'm walkin', ain't I?

SERA: Same as they gotta right to be growin' where they growin'.

(WALLY *has finally succeeded in untangling himself and is now stomping the sticka bush into the ground.*)

WALLY: There now! There! Who doin' what to who? Huh?! Who doin' who? Huh?! That'll teach ya not to come crawlin' up my legs, you goddamn sticka bush!

SERA: *(Arms folded and grim faced.)* You a travelin' man?

WALLY: Well, yeah, kinda. I move around alot.

SERA: That's what I figured.

WALLY: Now and then I stay in a place, but I don't never stay for long.

SERA: Figured that, too.

WALLY: I just ain't never found me a place I wanted to stay in for long.

SERA: I figured I'd seen the last of you when you left the diner. Figured you'd hitch you a ride outta here first thing.

WALLY: That's what I was aimin' on doin', but there weren't no cars passin'.

SERA: Hardly ever is.

WALLY: What's a diner doin' on a road where there ain't no cars passin'.

SERA: How'd you come in on that highway?

WALLY: I walked.

SERA: Then I guess that's your way out.

WALLY: Ain't there never no cars passin'?

SERA: Used to be lots of cars passin'.

WALLY: Yeah?

SERA: Used to be, but not no more.

WALLY: I stood out in front of that highway till I thought my brains were gonna bust right outta the top of my head.

SERA: Heat like this you oughta be wearin' a hat.

WALLY: I ain't got no hat.

SERA: Oughta be wearin' one anyway.

WALLY: If I had one I'd wear it.

SERA: Yeah, but you ain't got one.

WALLY: That's why I ain't wearin' it.

SERA: If you had you an honest job you could buy one.

WALLY: I ain't got no job.

SERA: Ain't got no hat, either.

WALLY: I don't want no hat.

SERA: If you found one layin' on the side of the road you'd pick it up quick enough.

WALLY: If it was layin' on the side of the road, yeah.

SERA: Then I guess you do want you a hat.

WALLY: I don't want no goddamn hat!

SERA: Then what the hell do you want!

WALLLY: What do you mean?

SERA: I wanna know what you doin' followin' after me.

WALLY: Well, I was gettin' 'round to that.

SERA: I'm listenin'.

WALLY: Like I said I was standin' out in front of the highway near dyin' from heat stroke—

SERA: No hat on your head, no wonder.

WALLY: *(Controlling his temper.)* —and I seen you leave the diner and come down this road.

SERA: What's where I'm walkin' got to do with anythin'?

WALLY: Well, when I seen you walkin' down this road I figured it might lead to somewhere.

SERA: Just an old dirt road don't lead nowhere.

WALLY: I saw you look back a couple of times, but you didn't say "get" so I figured it was alright.

SERA: Figured what was alright?

WALLY: I don't know. Just my followin' behind, I guess. You didn't say "get". —I figured maybe this road might lead to another highway.

SERA: Well, you figured wrong. It don't lead to no highway and it don't lead to no motel, neither. So you just go on and get.

WALLY: It's just I walked in on that highway. It took me all day and not a car come by. No, that ain't right. There was this one car, but he tried to run me down. Shouted somethin' through the window at me, but I didn't pay it no mind. I just kept on walkin'. All day of nothin' but walkin' and now I guess I gotta walk somemo'. *(Squints up at the sun.)*—I'm just hot, that's all. Hot and tired and—yeah, lookin' for company I got no right to. But I want you to know somethin'. I didn't mean you no harm. I don't mean nobody no harm. *(Wally turns and begins walking off.)*

SERA: Where you gonna go?

WALLY: Back to the highway, I guess.

SERA: You can go on back to the diner. Eddie ain't closed up yet.

WALLY: I done used up what money I had to buy that coffee with. I can't sit in that place without buyin' nothin'.

SERA: No, Eddie wouldn't allow that.

(A moment of awkward silence.)

SERA: I guess it be alright for you to sit a spell. It's a little cooler here than it is out on that highway. Not much, but some.

WALLY: Awh, thank you so much! I really appreciate it! I —

(WALLY advances on SERA quickly. She stumbles back defensively.)

SERA: Hold on! I didn't say make yourself to home. I just said you can sit a spell.

WALLY: *(Stops abruptly; smile faltering.)* Oh—sure—I'm sorry. I don't know what I did wrong, but I'm sorry. It just makes me feel good to be with somebody.

SERA: I don't like bein' with nobody. I don't even like bein' with myself 'cept there ain't too much I can do about that. *(A pause as SERA looks at WALLY'S downcast face.)* —I don't know what I did neither, boy, and I'm sorry, too. If you can figure out somethin' to smile about you go 'head and don't mind me. (WALLY'S *smile returning.*) Just do me a favor and don't be runnin' up on me all of a sudden, alright?

WALLY: Alright.

(SERA *goes and kneels in front of her garden. She picks and pulls at the weeds.* WALLY *sets his suitcase down, then pulls from his back pocket a stiff, wadded, checkered handkerchief which he uses to mop his sweating face and neck.*)

WALLY: It sure must be nice havin' a place in the woods like this.

SERA: This ain't no woods. A few pine trees don't make no woods. Used to be lots of trees but over the years I been here most all of 'em been cut down.

WALLY: This your trailer, huh?

SERA: I live in it, but it ain't mine. It belongs to Eddie. He just lets me stay in it.

(Thunder, low and distant.)

WALLY: Gonna rain!

SERA: That what you think?

WALLY: Looks like it.

SERA: Yeah, it looks like it.

WALLY: Makin' noises like it.

SERA: Doin' that, too.

WALLY: Well, don't that mean it gonna rain?

SERA: Not around here it don't.

WALLY: It gotta rain sometime.

SERA: Sometime it do. A lotta time it don't.

WALLY: I think this gonna be the sometime it do. I think it gonna rain.

ACT ONE SOME RAIN

SERA: I don't think nothin' no more. When the rain come down it be rainin'.

WALLY: And maybe cool things off, huh? Wouldn't that be nice? The rain just pourin' down coolin' everythin' off?

SERA: That sure would be nice everythin' dryin' up like it is. Used to have me a little garden here but it dried up.

WALLY: Ain't nothin' gonna grow in this heat.

SERA: Even the weeds are dyin'.

WALLY: That about all I come across around here is weeds. Weeds and sticka bushes. I ain't been able to walk ten feet without havin' to stop and pull 'em off me. My ankles about rubbed raw from them goddamn things.

SERA: I bought some flowers looked pretty on the seed package they come in. I planted 'em just like it said on the back, but they never did come up. Maybe I just wasn't around enough to water 'em proper. Sometimes even when I was here I'd forget or be too tired . . . Maybe that's why it ain't rained in so long. Maybe God gets tired too.

WALLY: Well, by the look of them clouds comin' on, he musta got him some sleep.

SERA: Yeah, sleep. That's what I figure them seeds are doin'. Sleepin' under the ground just waitin' for some rain to come along and wake 'em up.

WALLY: I tell you what you oughta do. You oughta plant you some of them sticka bushes in that there garden and I bet they be climbin' all over your trailer inside a week.

SERA: I don't see nothin' all that bad about a sticka bush. It's just a rose without the rose. Just leaves and thorns stickin' you, lettin' you know it's there even though it ain't pretty to look at. It's still there and lettin' you know it. Lettin' you know you there, too.

(A pause as SERA gets up from her garden and limps to the front steps of the trailer where she sits.)

SERA: Sometimes I be comin' home from work feelin' so tired I don't feel nothin' at all. A sticka bush come along it ain't in my way. It lettin' me know I'm there. —A body gotta feel somethin'. Pain better than no feelin' at all.

(WALLY *takes a step forward and trips over a piece of wood.*)

SERA: Watch yourself. There's nails in some of them boards. I stepped on one awhile back and it went clear through my foot. Swoll up like a balloon and blood and pus come out of it real bad so I could hardly walk.

WALLY: You didn't go to no hospital?

SERA: Nearest hospital is in Mobile and that's 34 miles from here. 'Sides I didn't have no money to pay 'em with. Eddie kept pleading with me to go, but I wouldn't. I soaked it every night in Epsom salts and after awhile it wasn't swoll up no more and there was just a little pus. It hurts sometimes so I gotta limp, but that's better than goin' to some hospital and havin' to pay 'em money I ain't got.

WALLY: You lucky you didn't get lock-jaw.

SERA: I guess.

WALLY: Ain't no guessin' about it. Why I had me this uncle once cut himself with a rusty knife he wasn't doin' nothin' but widdlin' with, and before he could turn around his jaw done locked up so tight all he could do to keep from starvin' was to suck mashed up food through his teeth. Lucky for him he had a few front ones missin'.

SERA: I didn't get no lock-jaw.

WALLY: Well, you could have.

SERA: I just limp some.

WALLY: I was wonderin' bout that. I seen you walkin' kind of funny. I just figured your shoes were too tight. (WALLY *kicks at a piece of wood.*) Why don't you clean this place up?

SERA: I been meanin' to for a long time now. I just ain't got around to it.

(WALLY *looks up at the sky, mopping his face and neck.*)

WALLY: You think with the sun goin' down it'd get cool.

SERA: Day and night it's the same. It don't never get better. You just get used to it.

WALLY: Yeah, it grows on you, I bet—like sticka bushes. You figure it's any cooler in the trailer?

SERA: I got me a fan inside, but it don't do much good.

WALLY: No, I don't guess it would. (WALLY *kicks his suitcase over on its side and sits down on top of it.*) It was nice and cool at the diner.

SERA: Yeah, some of the time. The air-conditioner is old though and breaks down a lot. Eddie bought it new, but that was a long time ago when I first come to work there. That was—lemme see—25 years ago.

WALLY: You been there that long?

SERA: Seems longer than that.

WALLY: Seems like forever to me. I ain't never stayed noplace for more than a year.

SERA: It was nice at first. Eddie's diner was right on the main highway and business was real good. But then the Interstate come through and changed all that. We don't get hardly no business no more.

WALLY: I noticed you weren't exactly packin' 'em in.

SERA: Mostly what we get now are strays. People who are lost, or ain't in no hurry to get noplace, or ain't got noplace to get to, anyhow.

WALLY: Who was that old sheriff-faced guy?

SERA: Who?

WALLY: The guy behind the counter looked like he'd been suckin' on a lemon.

SERA: Oh, Eddie. He owns the place.

WALLY: I seen a better lookin' face on the north end of a south bound mule.

SERA: Oh, he's o.k. It's just the bad business turned him sour.

WALLY: Well, it sure did one hell of a good job on him. (WALLY *takes off his t-shirt.*) Lord, this heat about to do me in. Look at this—soppin' wet. I can wring the sweat right out of it.

SERA: You sure got you some muscles.

WALLY: Yeah, the Lord gimme that much.

SERA: You must be pretty strong, huh?

WALLY: Well, I don't like to brag none, but I had me this job once workin' in a warehouse and I could work longer and lift more than anybody there. The boss man was all the time tellin' me how I was the best worker he ever had. Here, lemme show you somethin'.

(WALLY *gets up and goes to the oil barrel.*)

SERA: What you fixin' to do?

WALLY: Lift this here barrel.

SERA: You can't lift that.

WALLY: Betcha I can, too.

SERA: You gonna hurt yourself.

WALLY: No, I ain't. Watch.

SERA: That thing been sittin' there so long no tellin' what gonna crawl out from under it.

WALLY: Just so it ain't no sticka bush grab hold of me, I don't care.

(WALLY *lifts the barrel, holds it above his head, and stands there smiling proudly.*)

WALLY: See, I told you I could lift it!

(SERA *walks over to* WALLY *and looks down at the circle of dark, moist earth where the barrel had been resting.*)

SERA: Lordy, look at all them worms!

WALLY: To hell with the worms! Look at me!

SERA: *(Looking at* WALLY.*)* Yeah, you sure do got you some muscles. I can see 'em good now.

WALLY: *(Looking down at his chest.)* Pretty ain't they? I'm kind of partial to 'em myself. Step back, now. I don't wanna hurt you none when I set it down. (SERA *steps back and* WALLY *sets the barrel back down.*) —See? Nothin' to it. I could do that all day and not be bothered.

SERA: Can you put it back where it was?

WALLY: What?

SERA: The barrel.

WALLY: This whole place a junkyard. What's it matter where the damn thing settin'?

SERA: It's just them worms I was thinkin' about. The sun gonna kill 'em 'fore they have a chance to get back in the ground.

WALLY: I done lift this great big barrel up and held it above my head and you worried about worms?

SERA: I just like critters, that's all.

WALLY: *(Putting barrel back; sulking.)* Alright.

SERA: Thank you.

WALLY: *(Still sore.)* You welcome.

SERA: *(Mollifying.)* It was mighty impressin' how you picked that barrel up. I wouldn't think nobody could do that.

WALLY: *(The hurt almost fully healed.)* Yeah?

SERA: You really are strong.

WALLY: *(Healed and happy.)* I know what you mean. I impress myself sometimes!

(A moment of shared shy smiling, then SERA *turns and limps toward the trailer.)*

WALLY: You ain't goin' in yet, are you?

SERA: No, not just yet. I'm just gonna air the place out some. All closed up like it is it's gonna be hot as an oven inside.

(Having reached and mounted the trailer steps, SERA *takes a key from her apron pocket and uses it on a rather large padlock affixed to the front door.)*

WALLY: How come you lock it up?

SERA: I don't know. Ain't nothin' worth stealin'. Ain't never nobody around to do no stealin'. Seem like the less I got the more I'm afraid it gonna get taken from me.

*(*SERA *goes inside.* WALLY *walks about restlessly using his t-shirt to wipe the sweat from his face, neck, arms and chest.)*

WALLY: The only thing I ever had of value was this pocket contraption with all kindsa gadgets stuck inside so you could do just about anythin' with it. There was a fork and spoon you could eat with, somethin' to open cans and bottles with, a screwdriver, a scissors and, uh—oh yeah, there was this little magnifyin' glass, but it weren't no good. I tried to look at an ant with it, but by the time I got close enough to the ant to see good I'd done smashed the ant. Lemme see— *(*SERA *comes out of the trailer and sits on the steps.)* Hell, I done forgot what all was in there and some of the gadgets I never did figure out what they were good for. All I wanted when I walked in that hardware store was a knife, but when I set eyes on that contraption with all the different do-dads I couldn't resist.

SERA: What a thing like that cost you?

WALLY: Four dollars and thirty-five cents, but I didn't care. I was carryin' the first sizable amount of money I'd ever worked hard to get and it was just burnin' a hole right in my pocket. Wasn't till I'd already took it home with me and pulled out every last one of them gadgets that I discovered the one thing it didn't have was a knife. *(Drawing near the door of the trailer.)* Lordy, it is an oven in there!

SERA: That's the fan blowin' the hot air out. It oughta not be so bad after awhile. Then I'm goin' in.

(Thunder low and distant, but not as low or as distant as before.)

WALLY: That rain comin' closer.

SERA: Seems like it.

WALLY: If I had me some money I could go back to the diner. I could drink me some coffee till the rain got over with or a ride come along.

SERA: If it rains, Eddie gonna close the place up.

WALLY: The sign out front say 24 hours.

SERA: That was when business was good. It ain't that way no more.

WALLY: I ain't gonna be able to get me a ride outta here in the rain. I ain't never got me a ride when it was rainin'. All the times I tried all I ever got was wet.

SERA: *(Getting up to go inside.)* Well, I'm sorry, but there just ain't nothin' I can do about that.

WALLY: How 'bout if I did some work for ya?

SERA: What you figurin' to do?

WALLY: Anythin' need fixin'? I'm real good at fixin' things.

SERA: Everythin' 'round here broke beyond fixin'.

WALLY: Well, maybe I could do some paintin'.

SERA: Ain't no paint and even if there was it be no use slappin' it on some wood already gone rotten.

WALLY: Ain't there nothin' I can do?

SERA: Nothin' I know of.

WALLY: Well—thank you anyway.

(WALLY *picks up his suitcase, turns, and begins to walk off.*)

SERA: There is one thing.

WALLY: *(Turning back.)* Yeah?

SERA: This yard sure could stand a good cleanin'.

WALLY: *(Throws suitcase down.)* I'll do it!

SERA: Hold on, now!

WALLY: What?

SERA: I can't pay you much.

WALLY: That don't matter. Anythin' better than nothin'. Whatever you can afford is alright with me.

(WALLY *goes to the barrel, begins moving it, then stops.*)

WALLY: Awh, hell!

SERA: What's the matter?

WALLY: We forgettin' somethin'.

SERA: What's that?

WALLY: All your critter friends. Must be a million of 'em livin' up under all this junk.

SERA: Well, *(Squinting up at the sky.)* —the sun ain't as bad as it was.

WALLY: No, it ain't.

SERA: And night comin' on.

WALLY: And maybe some rain.

SERA: —Maybe.

WALLY: And I'll be real careful not to hurt them critters none.

SERA: That would be nice.

WALLY: Then I got me a job?

SERA: *(Turning and mounting the steps.)* If you do one thing first.

WALLY: *(Following to the edge of the steps, looking into the trailer where SERA has gone.)* What's that?

SERA: *(In the doorway of the trailer, holding out to WALLY an old, raggedy straw hat.)* Put this hat on your head.

WALLY: *(Taking the hat.)* Lady, you just hired you some help!

(WALLY *puts on the hat, then beams an engagingly boyish smile.* SERA, *before she realizes it, is smiling back. It isn't all that much of a smile from a definite lack of practice, but the interesting change here is that she doesn't grunt or grimace it away. She leaves it there while continuing to watch* WALLY *as he begins his work.*)

WALLY: *(Having just moved the old oil barrel, he looks down at where it had been resting.)* Alright little poppa critter and momma critter, get your chilrun together and pack up your bags cuz it's movin' time!

(Abrupt darkness.)

END OF ACT I, SCENE I

A flash of lightning. A rumble of closely attendant thunder. An hour has passed and though the clouds have continued their advance, the sun has in no way retreated. A conflagration of colliding colors create a cathedral effect: harsh light through dark glass.

WALLY *can be seen putting the finishing touches on his labor. His naked upper torso, gleaming with sweat, reflects the rainbow hues of the savage sky. The ground has been cleared and he is now sweeping it clean. All the trash has been neatly stacked in a pile to the rear.*

There is a yellowish glare of light issuing from the trailer door as well as a small curtained window. SERA *can be seen passing in front of this window and she can be heard humming a pleasant tune.*

After a moment, a single, bare bulb above the trailer door is switched on and SERA *comes out carrying a tray with a pitcher of iced lemonade and two glasses. She has changed from her waitress uniform to a simple but becoming house dress, has applied some light make-up, and has unpinned and combed her hair. One can now see that she was, indeed, young once and pretty in her own way. She stands immobile at the top of the steps completely captivated by the sky.* WALLY *goes on with his sweeping unaware of her presence.*

WALLY: *(About to sweep, stops, then squints down at the ground.)* Come on little critter, has you got to be crawlin' just where I'm sweeping?

(SERA'S *gaze drops from the sky to* WALLY.)

WALLY: *(Nudging the bug with the broom.)* Come on, bug, I got work to do. All your family and friends have done moved. They all over there where the junk is. *(Pointing.)* See? *(The bug obviously doesn't.)* No, not that way, that way! *(He nudges the bug again.)* I think you don't rightly understand just how close you are to gettin' scrunched up under my foot. I think if you realized that you'd be haulin' ass outta my way. *(The bug pays no attention to the threat and* WALLY, *completely losing patience, sweeps the bug away harshly.)* Oh, the hell with it!

(WALLY *looks up, sees* SERA, *freezes a moment, then slams the broom then the hat down on the ground.)*

WALLY: Goddamn! You done ruined me, you know that? I ain't gonna be able to walk straight no more without fearin' I'm mashin' some goddamn bug ain't got the sense not to be crawlin' where I'm walkin'.

SERA: *(Coming down the steps.)* Never mind that. Come on and get some of this lemonade I fixed 'fore it all turns to water. You must be hot.

WALLY: *(Grabbing his t-shirt up off the ground, he uses it to wipe the sweat from his face, neck, arms and chest as he walks over to* SERA.) Hot?! I'm burnin' up! I'm on fire! I'm madder than a bob cat! Just lemme lay eyes on one more goddamn bug and see what I do. Do I reach down and shake hands with it, say "Good mornin' Mr. Bug" or "Good evenin' Mrs. Bug"? No sir! I'm gonna stomp down on it so fast you be able to hear its guts poppin' from here to Georgia!

SERA: *(Pouring lemonade.)* Here.

WALLY: Thank you.

SERA: You welcome

(WALLY *takes the glass, then sits down on the ground near the steps. He begins scratching himself here and there.* SERA *puts the tray down on the steps, then sits.)*

WALLY: And them goddamn sticka bushes! They worse than the bugs. Every time I reached up behind somethin' to grab hold of it, some goddamn sticka bush grabbed me back.

SERA: I'm sorry.

WALLY: I got 'em back though. I took me that shovel of yours and I beat 'em down, then I dug 'em up.

SERA: They be grow'd back in the mornin'

WALLY: Yeah, well, I give 'em hell, anyway. I done 'em that.

(As WALLY gulps down his lemonade, SERA looks up at the sky.)

SERA: I ain't never seen the sky look like that before.

(WALLY wipes his mouth with the back of his hand while looking up at the sky. He continues, as he has been doing, unmindfully scratching himself here and there.)

WALLY: Yeah, it's gonna rain, alright. Just my luck to get caught between here and nowhere, and get wet besides. *(WALLY finally becomes aware of his itching and scratching.)* Them goddamned bugs bit the shit out of me!

(SERA reaches a hand to WALLY'S chest. She runs her fingers over one insect bite, then another. After a moment she takes her hand away, gets up from the steps and walks into the yard.)

SERA: You done a fine piece of work on this yard. It make me feel bad I can't pay you near as good as the job you done.

WALLY: That's alright. Like I tole you before, anythin' better than nothin'.

SERA: I was watchin' you before. Watchin' you work. It kind of reminded me of myself when I was young and business at Eddie's was good. I'd be carryin' 6 plates with one hand and wipin' down a table with the other. Movin' around like I was wearin' roller skates and not payin' nothin' no mind 'cept my work and how good I was doin' it. There was a satisfaction in it I couldn't get nowhere else.

WALLY: Make you some money?

SERA: Lordy, did I! When business was good them tips was sweet. And young and foolish as I was I wasn't lookin' to save a penny of it neither. What I couldn't buy out of the mail order catalog I had Eddie drive me to town to buy. Had me clothes I didn't never wear. Had me a car almost new. Had me a house I was payin' on, pictures to put on the walls, and brand new furniture. Had me a TV, a radio and a record player, too. Had me more things than I can remember havin', and all of it gone now.

WALLY: What happened?

SERA: A flood come along and washed it all way. Not long after that the Interstate come through and ruined all of Eddie's business. Ain't nothin' left now—'cept that feelin' I remember havin' when I was doin' good what it was I was doin'. Waitressin' ain't nothin' special, but by God I was the best Eddie's diner ever seen or ever will see.

WALLY: I bet you was a fine waitress.

SERA: *(Returning to steps.)* Bless your heart, I was. I truly was. Now I'm old and slow and don't hardly care about nothin'. The only thing keep the customers from yellin' at me is their feelin' sorry cuz of my limp.

WALLY: You figure you might get fired?

SERA: What? Eddie fire me? Not a snowball's chance in hell. As bad as I've gotten I'm still better than any girl Eddie's hired in a long time, and he's hired a bunch of 'em. The trouble is they don't stay. As quick as he hires 'em they run off. Just ain't no money to be made in that place no more and them girls can see it right off.

WALLY: If it's as bad as all that, why don't you get out?

SERA: For the same reason I don't get fired, I guess. Just ain't somethin' to be done no more. Been there too long. Done too much for Eddie and him for me. Guess I'm gonna wind up dyin' there. Won't that be a pretty picture for the papers: layin' out on the floor 'tween the tables at Eddie's diner with peas and carrots and mashed potatoes all over me, and a poke chop layin' up aside my head.

WALLY: Well, you ain't gotta worry about nothin' like that happenin' for a long time.

SERA: You just fulla sweet talk, ain't ya?

WALLY: No sweet talk about it. You still a young woman.

SERA: That's nice of you to say, but it ain't so. I ain't young no more. I ain't even alive no more.

WALLY: What do you mean by that?

SERA: I mean I don't havta spend no time worryin' over when I'm gonna croak cuz it already happened.

WALLY: That don't make no sense.

SERA: Yes, it does. I feel it inside me like I see it inside some people who come into the diner and it ain't got nothin' to do with how old you are. Some time in your life, for some reason or other, you lay down inside yourself and that's that. You still go on gettin' up in the mornin', still go to work, still keep on with whatever it is you life has you to do, but it ain't like you alive no more. Inside you done laid down and that's that.

WALLY: I seen my Granny die. Heard her makin' noises in her throat. Her eyes wide open like she was lookin' at somethin' fearful ugly. I went cryin' down the road to Miss Manard's house, but there weren't nothin' she could do. Weren't nothin' nobody could do.

SERA: That's how it is alotta times—nothin' nobody can do.

WALLY *takes an ice cube from his glass and rubs it over his face, neck, arms and chest.)*

SERA: *(Looking up at the clouds.)* If it comin' down it gonna be soon.

WALLY: Just so it cools things off some. I feel like I'm on fire.

SERA: Where you from?

WALLY: *(Pouring himself another glass of lemonade.)* Georgia. Only I ain't been back there in a long time. I move around alot. Like I said before I can't seem to stay in one place. Gotta keep movin'.

SERA: You runnin' away from somethin'?

WALLY: I ain't in no trouble with the law, if that's what you mean.

SERA: The law ain't the only thing chase after a man.

WALLY: I just—

SERA: What?

WALLY: I don't know. Like somethin' ain't right. I want—I want so bad, so much, and I don't know what it is I want. It's movin' till I'm movin', then movin' ain't it. It's stayin' in one place till I've stayed a while and seen that ain't it. It's wantin' what I ain't got till I get it, then I don't want it no more. It's all the time dreamin' till I grab ahold of what it is I'm dreamin' for and when I open my eyes it's gone.

SERA: Sound like a dog chasin' after his own tail.

WALLY: Ain't no such thing. I'm just lookin' for somethin'.

SERA: What?

WALLY: That's what I ain't figured out, yet.

SERA: All that figurin' is in your head, boy. Livin' is different.

WALLY: I don't see why it's gotta be.

SERA: It ain't gotta be. It is. What you lookin' for don't exist. That's why it ain't no place to be found.

WALLY: Well, I'm just gonna keep lookin' anyway, and I ain't gonna stop till I find it.

SERA: A dog chasin' after his own damn tail.

WALLY:(*Up and moving about.*) Ain't you just like my Granny! Ain't ya just like her, now. She was all the time tryin' to set me straight about livin' with what is. Not what you think oughta be. Not no wishes. And not no dreams. That ain't nothin' but the devil temptin' you. What is, that's what you gotta live with, but—I got crazy dreams 'bout my Momma. "You can be anybody you wanna be. Do anythin' you set your mind to do." And I don't know if it's a dream or me remembering Momma. I don't know whether to love her or hate her. I get to thinkin' I'm somethin' better than nothin' and I get to runnin' and as long as I'm runnin' I ain't gotta be nothin' or know nothin'. The world just go whizzin' by and I'm free!—

Then the car stop and the world standin' still again. The door open up and I'm right back where I started from: standin' on the side of the road with nowhere to go, nothin' to do, and nobody to be with.

SERA: Your Momma still livin'?

WALLY: *(Hangs his head, shakes it "No")* —She died from drinkin'.

SERA: Where your Poppa at?

WALLY: He run off when I was still inside my Momma. He took one look at that belly gettin' big and he was gone.

SERA: Then your Granny raised you up?

WALLY: If you can call livin' in hell bein' raised up.

SERA: Bad as all that?

WALLY: Worse. All the time workin' my ass off and woopin' me for what seemed like no reason at all. All the time readin' her bible and sayin' her prayers and me all the time wishin' she'd die and go to hell. Even the kids what lived down the road that she wouldn't never let me play with, whenever they passed the house they'd throw rocks at it. Then she died and people come from miles around to be at her funeral. More people than I'd ever seen before in one place at one time. And all of 'em cryin' and sayin' what a wonderful woman she was, so I didn't know what to think. She wasn't never nothin' but mean to me.

SERA: Maybe what you took to be mean was her way of lovin'.

WALLY: I don't know. I still think on it sometimes. I remember we had this old tom cat what always hung around and if I didn't sneak him some scraps now and then he wouldn't of never got fed. Seemed like Granny had about as little use for him as she had for me. Come to think of it, he didn't seem too partial to her neither. Mostly what they did was just stay out of each other's way. Then one day that tom cat dug up some fish bones I'd buried out back and got one of 'em stuck in his throat so he couldn't breathe. Well, when Granny caught sight of it through the kitchen window she dropped the taters she was peelin' and run out the back door after that old tom cat like I never seen her run before. When she got to him she grabbed him up by his neck and pinned him 'tween her knees and proceeded to pry his mouth open. Well, that old tom cat was as puzzled as I was over what she had a mind to do and what with that bone jammed in his throat I guess he figured he didn't need no trouble from her besides, so he commenced to claw Granny's arms up till the blood was just pourin' down her apron. Well, she never paid it no mind and just kept on with what she was doin' till she'd pried that tom cat's mouth wide open and shoved her hand down his throat. Pretty soon her hand come out again and she had that fish bone 'tween her fingers. Then she threw him on the ground and kicked him so he jumped up and ran off like a pack of hounds was on his tail. *(Touched by the memory; confused.)* —She had no use for that tom cat yet she saved his life. Kept him livin' when he should have been dead. I guess that's a kind of lovin'.

SERA: Sure it is.

WALLY: When she died I set out on my own. Been on my own ever since.

(Lightning flash followed closely by thunder, long and loud. The wind picks up.)

SERA: *(Stands, looks up at the sky.)* Can you smell it?

WALLY: Yeah, it gonna rain, alright.

SERA: I knew it would, but then I didn't. Didn't let myself believe.

WALLY: *(Picks up the broom and hat, leans the broom against the trailer, then hands the hat to* SERA.*)* If you pay me for what work I done I'll be on my way.

SERA: It fixin' to rain any minute.

WALLY: Ain't too much I can do about that.

SERA: You welcome to stay in my trailer till the rain over with.

WALLY: You mean it?

SERA: Give you a chance to rest up and get somethin' to eat. I noticed you didn't eat nothin' at the diner.

WALLY: I didn't have no money but what I could buy coffee with.

SERA: Well, I got dinner on the stove right now. And I could wash your shirt out in the sink and hang it to dry in front of the fan. It'd be ready in no time.

WALLY: I can't pay you for it.

SERA: The job you done on this yard more than pay for it. You ain't gotta worry about owin' me nothin'.

(*As the rain begins to fall,* WALLY *gathers his things together.* SERA *descends the steps and walks out into the yard.*)

WALLY: You gonna get wet.

SERA: That's what I aim on doin'. You go on in, now. I'll be there in a minute.

(WALLY *stops at the trailer door. He turns back and watches* SERA.)

SERA: (*To herself, the sky and the falling rain.*) I just gotta be in it awhile and let it come down all over me. O—o—o—h, that feels so good. When it's been dry this long a body need some rain.

(SERA *in the rain.* WALLY *watching her from the trailer door. Lightning and thunder. Lights fade.*)

END OF ACT I, SCENE II

ACT II

The yard is in darkness. The rain falls steady with occasional lightning and thunder. The front side of the trailer has been removed to expose the dimly lit, cramped and squalid quarters of the interior. Dinner has been eaten. SERA *and* WALLY *are seated at a small table in the center. There is a half empty bottle of whisky on the table.*

WALLY *is wearing, what is for him, a dress or fancy shirt which he has taken from his suitcase. Even in its present frayed and faded condition it is loudly colorful. His hair is slicked back and he is slouching comfortably in his chair with his legs spread widely apart. The t-shirt which he wore in the beginning of the first act has been washed and is now hanging in front of a small, droning and erratically turning fan.*

The lights rise on WALLY *telling a story. He is very excited and animated.* SERA *is laughing.*

WALLY: So I'm pullin' the net in—just two days out and I don't know the front of the trawler from the back—and pullin' that old net in, and most all we got is catfish and they ain't worth the time it takes to bother with 'em, and I'm tired and gettin' real mad at this one catfish caught up in the net so bad a stick of dynamite wouldn't turn him loose, and the old Cap'n half pie-eyed and screamin' down my neck curses I ain't never even heard before. So all I can see is red and this goddamn catfish what's causin' me all this trouble so I slam him down on the deck.

SERA: The Captain?

WALLY: No, not the Cap'n, the goddamn catfish!

SERA: Oh—h—h!

WALLY: So I slam him down on the deck figurin' to jar him loose from the net and his eyes are rollin' around like this. (WALLY *rolls his eyes comically.* SERA *is beside herself with laughter.*)

SERA: Go on and stop now 'fore I bust a gut.

WALLY: But as much as his eyes are rollin', he's still caught up in the net worse than ever and now I'm nearly as mad at that worthless catfish as the Cap'n is at me for bein' such a worthless deck hand, so I go to kick him.

SERA: The Captain?

WALLY: No, the goddamn catfish!

SERA: Oh—h—h!

WALLY: And as much as he's caught up in the net he's still wigglin' around like a worm in the rain. Wigglin' like this. (WALLY *wiggles comically.* SERA'S *laughter is renewed.*)

SERA: Stop, Wally! Stop! I can't laugh no more!

WALLY: So I go to kick the goddamn catfish, slip, and its spike goes right through my sneaker and nips the end of my toe. And everybody, includin' the Cap'n, laughin' their asses off cuz I'm all of a sudden dancin' around like I done stepped in an ant pile. Like this. (WALLY *gets up and dances around comically.* SERA *tries to keep from laughing, but can't. With both arms she holds her aching sides.*)

SERA: Wally, stop it now! I can't laugh no more without it hurtin' me. Wally! Sit down now and finish your story.

WALLY: *(Sits.)* So now I'm really mad and gonna get that bastard if it's the last thing I do, so I take me a knife and I'm gonna stick him.

SERA: You didn't!

WALLY: Didn't what?

SERA: Stick the Captain.

WALLY: No, not the Cap'n, the goddamn catfish!

SERA: Oh—h—h!

WALLY: *(Squinting an eye at* SERA.) You funnin' me, ain't ya? (SERA *tries to keep a straight face, but can't. She bursts into laughter.)* Yeah, I guess it is funny, but I sure wasn't laughin' then. All I wanted to do was stick that goddamn catfish and when I went to do it, I missed and his spike catches me again right through my glove and into my finger all the way to the bone.

SERA: Oh no, Wally!

WALLY: As God is my witness. Well, then I really started yellin': "Cap'n!" But that old Cap'n about wise to me now and he know what I know ain't nothin' about bein' on a Shrimper. And he callin' back, "What you botherin' me with now you lyin' land walker! Stop playin' with them cats and pull in them shrimp!" "Cap'n!" I screamed, "I got a catfish stuck in my finger!" "Well, pull it out!", he says. "I can't, Cap'n, its too deep!" So he comes over to take a look at it and right away he could see I wasn't lyin' cuz my glove was full of blood pourin' over the sides. And that old Cap'n was right pleased like I been baptized or somethin' and become a true shrimper. It took a pair of pliers and a hell of alot of pullin' to get that catfish to let go of my finger.

SERA: What happened to the catfish?

WALLY: That about what beat all. Once he'd been pulled from my finger he wiggled free of the net and jumped back into the water. I seen him swim off like nothin' happened and I'm standin' there bleedin' to death.

SERA: Your finger got alright, didn't it?

WALLY: Oh, yeah. The Cap'n fixed it up real good and him and me almost got to be friends after that. If it hadn't been for some guy I couldn't get along with bein' hired on I guess I'd still be there. Somethin' about bein' on water like movin' on land. There was times I was almost at peace. Other times there was enough work to keep me from wonderin' why there wasn't no peace.

SERA: I'm glad that catfish got away.

WALLY: Yeah, lookin' back on it now, me too. He didn't mean no harm. Just got himself caught up in somethin' he didn't know nothin' about. *(A pause of smiling rememberance, then laughter.)* —Ooh, the stories I could tell you about that old Shrimper.

SERA: Not right now, Wally. Please. I gotta give my belly a rest. I ain't used to laughin' like I been doin'. I don't know when I've laughed so much.

WALLY: I can see laughin's good for you. You look different somehow then you did before.

SERA: How is it I look now?

WALLY: You look pretty.

SERA: *(Blushing.)* This rain must be coolin' things off. I don't know why I feel so hot.

WALLY: *(Drawing near.)* You got you a tin roof. That don't help none.

SERA: No, it don't.

(WALLY *kisses* SERA. *For a moment* SERA *lingers, then draws away.*)

WALLY: What's the matter?

SERA: Nothin'.

WALLY: Then how come you pull away like that?

SERA: It's just—

WALLY: What?

SERA: *(Gathering dishes.)* I gotta do these dishes.

WALLY: I thought you wanted me to kiss you.

SERA: I thought so, too.

WALLY: And now you don't.

SERA: *(Taking dishes to the sink.)* Now I don't know.

WALLY: *(Following.)* So what's the matter? Ain't I good lookin' enough?

SERA: You about as good lookin' as I seen a man be.

WALLY: Then what's the matter?

SERA: I told you I don't know. Just lemme do these dishes.

WALLY: Alright, do the damn dishes.

(WALLY *goes to the door and stands there looking out at the rain. There is a moment of silence between* SERA *and* WALLY, *the silence filled with the sound of the steadily falling rain.*)

SERA: I'm at the diner so much I don't hardly feel right less I got some dishes in my hands. I'm at the diner 8, 10 hours a day, but alot of times the young girls Eddie hires don't show so I gotta work their shift, too. Them young girls ain't lookin' for work. The first guy comes along talks nice to 'em they jump in his car and they're gone. Can't blame 'em none. This ain't no place to be.

WALLY: Was when you was younger.

SERA: Yeah.

WALLY: Said you was makin' good money.

SERA: More than enough to keep my ears closed to alot of sweet talk.

WALLY: Lots of men wanted to take you with 'em I bet.

SERA: Some.

WALLY: And you wouldn't listen.

SERA: I always figured there'd be one come along different from all the rest. He'd walk into Eddie's and I'd know he was the one.

WALLY: And he never come.

SERA: If he did it was on my day off. —Guess my nose was

kind of high in the air then. By the time I'd stopped bein' so particular there weren't nobody askin' me to go nowhere 'cept back to the kitchen to get 'em another order of fries.

WALLY: *(Walking, looking around.)* This ain't such a bad place, Sera.

SERA: I guess. I didn't like it none at first. It was quite a disappointment after losin' my house in the flood, but I've gotten used to it. The trailer belongs to Eddie and since business got so bad he don't charge me no rent. No rent is about all I can afford to pay right now.

WALLY: *(Sitting back down, pouring himself a drink.)* I've lived in worse places.

SERA: I used to think about movin' on by myself and not wait for nobody to take me. I used to think about it alot, but I kept puttin' it off. Now there ain't nowhere I wanna go. I'm settled.

WALLY: What you got here ain't bad.

SERA: *(Drying her hands with a dish towel, looking about resignedly.)* No, it ain't bad, but—what I was thinkin' was how much better things would be if there was someone to come home to. Like when I had that dog I found out in front of Eddie's. He'd been hit by a car but I nursed him real good till he was all better. He was a darlin' little dog all brown and white. He was—he was someone to come home to.

WALLY: You don't have him no more?

SERA: When he got better he run off and I never seen him again.

(SERA *goes back to the table and sits. She pours herself a drink.*)

SERA: That flood I told you about was 8–9 years ago, and the rain come down hard like it's comin' down now only it didn't let up till the whole area was flooded. I spent days helpin' Eddie bail out the Diner, then I come home and home wasn't there no more. That's when Eddie fixed it so I could move in here.

WALLY: Somethin' between you and him?

SERA: I don't know. Nothin' that was ever spoken. I mean—I've done for him and him for me, things you wouldn't hardly do for nobody, but—weren't nothin' romantic. Just friends, I guess. Good friends.

WALLY: I don't like him.

SERA: You don't know him.

WALLY: I seen him at the Diner.

SERA: Take more time then that to know somebody.

WALLY: Seen him lookin' to make sure I had me some money 'fore he'd pour my coffee. Seen him eyein' me like I was trash.

SERA: Awh, that ain't nothin' to judge him by.

WALLY: He was judgin' me, wasn't he?

SERA: It's just since business got so bad he's changed some. I can tell you from knowin' him a long time ain't no finer man around. He'd give you the shirt off his back if that's what you needed from him.

WALLY: He sure wasn't lookin' to give me none of that watered down coffee. He stood there watchin' while I counted out every cent in my pocket. Made me feel cheap.

(WALLY *angrily downs his drink and pours another.*)

SERA: That's what the bad business has done to him. Weren't like that before. When times was good there was them that could pay and them that couldn't didn't have to. Now thing's so bad he gotta turn people away his heart wants to help. That's why his face is all twisted up. Not cuz he mean. Cuz he gotta heart love to give and there ain't nothin' left to give. *(Pause.)* You ever been married, Wally?

WALLY: No.

SERA: You never had you nobody special?

WALLY: I ain't no good with women.

SERA: I can't believe that.

WALLY: It's true.

SERA: You a good lookin' boy.

WALLY: I ain't sayin' women ain't attracted to me. Everywhere I go I run into women lookin' to get close to me.

SERA: Don't you want to get close to them?

WALLY: Well, sure, but—

SERA: What?

WALLY: It just don't seem right.

SERA: People being attracted to each other?

WALLY: No, not that. That seem only natural. It's wantin' what you got between you to last forever. *(Pause.)* I had me this girl once. I had a powerful feeling for her, but she didn't want to leave where she was to go nowhere, and all the lovin' we had between us wasn't enough to keep me from movin' on. I know it ain't no good. I know it ain't gettin' me nowhere. I just can't seem to stay put.

SERA: You gotta settle down sometime.

WALLY: Like you gotta die sometime. When I ain't movin' no more is when I be buried.

SERA: If you wanted to, you could stay here for awhile.

WALLY: You mean for the night?

SERA: I mean for awhile.

WALLY: How long is that?

SERA: Longer than a night.

WALLY: I can't stay nowhere, Sera. I just got done tellin' you that.

SERA: You could look for work.

WALLY: I'd be afraid I'd find it.

(A pause as SERA *pours herself another drink.)*

SERA: Sometimes when I been workin' all day and come home I need a drink just to feel right.

WALLY: Why don't you do somethin' besides waitressin'?

SERA: Waitressin' is all I know how to do, but I'm gettin' old and bein' on my feet all the time ain't no good. Sometimes my legs hurt so bad I can't sleep.

WALLY: Yeah, well, there ain't too much I can do about that.

SERA: I'm all the time alone 'cept when I took care of that dog, but he run off. Oh, I used to think there was somethin' between Eddie and me. For a long time after I went to work for him I'd be doin' somethin' and look up sudden and he'd be lookin' at me like I weren't wearin' no clothes. Then when I look again he done turned away and busied himself doin' this or that. Alotta times I caught him like that, lookin' at me with somethin' strange in his eyes, then makin' like I wasn't there at all. I always figured he was just shy and slow to come 'round, but in all the years I know'd him, he ain't never come 'round. *(Pause.)* I just work, that's all, it's all I know how to do. Sometimes I work even when I don't have to cuz I don't know what else to do with myself. I'm savin' up all my money now so I can get me a TV. What I don't spend on food and stuff I put away and once it's there I don't touch it for nothin', not even when I need the money bad. I need me that TV bad. I need somethin' to come home to. I'm all the time alone, Wally, all the time and—I can't hardly stand it no more.

*(*SERA *runs out of the trailer crying.* WALLY *at a loss. He runs a hand through the curliness of his hair. He reaches for the bottle, then stops. He looks toward the door, the blackness beyond it, and the suffering that has just passed through it. He walks to the door, squints out into the impenetrable darkness, then searches 'round the door*

frame for the outside-light switch.

When the light comes on, SERA *is seen kneeling in the mud before her garden silently weeping. The rain has, for the moment and the most part, abated. All the creatures, creepers and crawlers of the night, are in boisterous celebratory song. A night offering to the god of rain.*

WALLY *descends the steps of the trailer.)*

WALLY: You o.k.?

SERA: I just need me some room to breathe.

WALLY: That trailer is small.

SERA: It ain't just the trailer. It's my life. There just ain't noplace I can go. I can't go back and change nothin'. I'm stuck where I am, stuck with who I am. Everyday is the same and it gonna stay that way till—

WALLY: Why don't you leave? Why don't you just pack what you got or don't even bother. Just get up and leave!

SERA: I can't do that.

WALLY: Why not?

SERA: I can't leave Eddie.

WALLY: What has that man ever done for you to make you feel married to him when y'ain't? What the hell has he ever done for you? Let you move into this shoebox? Slave ya day after day for weeks and months and years of your life? Them years are gone, Sera, and whadda ya got? Nothin'. That what he give ya: Nothin'.

SERA: I've known Eddie for years and I've seen him many a time tryin' to be better than what he is, tryin' and fallin', then gettin' himself up again so he can try somemo'. I've seen him needin' and not knowin' how to need, not knowin' what to do with it 'cept hide it up inside him like it were somethin' dirty. In his own way he's made love to me and just because he's been thoughtless and careless in the way he's gone about it don't make him no worse than any other man. I just wish once, just once he'd of said somethin'. —Oh, that ain't so. He's tole me he loves me lots of times. He just never used no words to do it with.

WALLY: I know his kind. All ya gotta do is look at him. Like he ain't never smiled and if he ever did his whole face would crack up and fall to pieces. I seen lotsa them faces: sheriffs and bosses and bullies. Nothin' but fools, all of 'em. Not one of 'em worth a damn and the world be better off without 'em.

SERA: 'He gotta right to be alive! Ain't no critter God put on this earth ain't gotta right to be here! Eddie mighta grow'd up crooked but he ain't no crime!

(In disregard of the mud and slush, WALLY crouches down behind SERA, balancing himself on his knees. He warmly and consolingly embraces her, resting his cheek on the back of her neck.)

WALLY: You sweet on that old sourpuss, ain't ya?

(SERA'S reply is a release of tears. A moment more of caressing, rocking, and WALLY'S head snaps up, his eyes dart about and he is smiling.)

WALLY: Sera? *(No answer. He shakes her excitedly.)* Sera!

SERA: What is it?

WALLY: Hear that?

SERA: What?

WALLY: The critters.

SERA: *(Wiping the tears from her eyes.)* God bless 'em.

WALLY: Singin'!

SERA: What they got to sing about I don't know.

WALLY: They know.

SERA: Well, I guess you gotta be a critter to figure that one out.

WALLY: Ain't you ever felt like singin'?

SERA: You mean like when you take a shower?

WALLY: I mean when your heart is so full of feelin' you gotta let it out. (WALLY *jumps up and starts singing at the top of his lungs.*) LA–LA–LA–LA–LA–LA–LA—

SERA: *(Amazed.)* What are you doin'?

WALLY: Singin'! LA–LA–LA–LA–LA—

SERA: *(Smiling.)* You crazy.

WALLY: Sometimes it helps. LA–LA–LA–LA–LA— (SERA *begins to laugh.*) Or dancin'!

(WALLY *jumps and twirls around the muddy yard. He slips and slides, falls and laughs, then he's up again, dancing again, jumping and twirling again.*)

SERA: *(Hesitant; low.)* la–la–la—

WALLY: That's it!

(WALLY *splashes over to* SERA, *takes her hand and pulls her up.*)

WALLY: Now, let's see if you can shake a leg.

SERA: Do what?

WALLY: Dance.

SERA: Oh, no, Wally. I can't. I don't know how.

WALLY: That don't matter none. I don't know how neither.

SERA: No, Wally, my leg—

(SERA *has turned to move away.* WALLY, *still holding on to her, pulls her back suddenly, embraces her tightly and kisses her passionately. A moment of near resistance and* SERA *returns the kiss.*)

WALLY: Dance with me, Sera.

SERA: *(Frightened; confused.)* I—

WALLY: What, Sera?

SERA: I gotta go to work in the mornin'.

WALLY: That's tomorrow.

SERA: *(Trying to pull away.)* Wally, please.

WALLY: *(Holding onto her gently.)* What?

SERA: I ain't never done nothin' like this before.

WALLY: That's yesterday.

SERA: Wally?

WALLY: Yes, Sera.

SERA: In the mornin' you be gone.

WALLY: There ain't no mornin' to it, Sera. No yesterday, today or tomorrow. Just now. Right now. You—and me— *(Looks up laughing at the renewal of rain.)* and some rain.

(SERA *and* WALLY *circle the yard in a dance of their own creation. The rain falls softly. Darkness slowly descends.*)

END OF ACT II, SCENE I

The following morning. The sun is shining, birds are singing and there is little if any visible evidence that it ever rained. Inside the trailer SERA *is asleep. She is alone. She stirs, yawning and stretching contentedly. Still half asleep she calls* WALLY'S *name. A moment and she is more awake, more fearful:* "WALLY?!" SERA *rises quickly and searches for* WALLY, *but he is nowhere to be found. As she moves about the trailer, the dragging hem of her nightgown catches trippingly at her limping leg. Finally she sits. With her elbows supported by the table, her hands support and cover her face.* SERA *cries. A moment and the sound of an approaching car is heard. It is an old car. It coughs and sputters to a stop. Another moment and* EDDIE *is seen approaching. He stops abruptly, startled over what was little more than a dump and is now a cleared area of land.*

EDDIE *is 55 years old, tall, thin and stoop shouldered. What's left of his hair is sandy grey and seems to have a mind of its own. Some of it lies this way and some of it that way and some of it, particularly a cow-lick at the back, stands straight up. His jaw is determined, but unsettled. A moment of time, a movement of cheek, and the determination fades and must be constantly reasserted. The pursing of his lips helps him accomplish this. His movements are awkward and uncertain, his summer suit wrinkled and ill-fitting, his hat weather stained and sun bleached. He squints his watery blue eyes constantly, having needed glasses for years. He has quite an eagle's beak of a nose and large, wrinkled hands he's never quite sure what to do with.*

EDDIE: Sera?

(No answer. EDDIE *takes a clean white handkerchief from his pocket, then removes his hat. He wipes first his forehead, then the sweat band of his hat. He puts his hat back on.)*

EDDIE: Sera, you in there?

(Inside the trailer SERA *raises her head and wipes her eyes with her hands. She quickly rises and clears the empty bottle of whiskey and glasses from the table. Outside* EDDIE *moves closer to the trailer door while putting his handkerchief away.)*

EDDIE: Sera?

SERA: What you want, Eddie?

EDDIE: You o.k.?

SERA: Yeah, I'm o.k.

(SERA *goes to the door. Upon seeing her,* EDDIE *immediately takes off his hat and averts his eyes. As he speaks he works his hat 'round and 'round in his hands.*)

EDDIE: When it come time for you to be to work and you weren't, I figured you were sick.

SERA: Twenty-five years of bein' on time you probably figured I was dead.

EDDIE: Sera! I'd never think nothin' like that. I just figured maybe you weren't feelin' too good.

SERA: I've felt better.

EDDIE: *(Squinting about him.)* I can't believe the change that's come over this yard.

SERA: I hired somebody.

EDDIE: Was it that boy I saw followin' after you last night?

SERA: Weren't no boy.

EDDIE: No, I don't guess he was.

SERA: Don't guess it's any of your business either.

EDDIE: No, I don't guess it is. (EDDIE *turns and takes a step to leave, then turns back.*) Sera?

SERA: What is it, Eddie?

EDDIE: You alright?

SERA: Why wouldn't I be alright?

EDDIE: I don't know. Somethin' in your voice—like you been cryin'.

SERA: It's just a cold I got. Must have been the rain last night give it to me.

(SERA *wipes the last of the tears from the corners of her eyes then comes out and sits on the steps. She blinks up at the sky.*)

EDDIE: That sure was some rain, wasn't it, Sera?

SERA: Yeah.

EDDIE: What little business I got left in the evening and that rain run it all off.

SERA: Did the Diner flood any?

EDDIE: Some.

SERA: You want me to help you clean it up?

EDDIE: I was hopin' you would.

SERA: O.K, Eddie, just lemme rest here for a minute 'fore I put that uniform back on. Seem like I just took it off.

EDDIE: You wanna ride back?

SERA: That's alright, Eddie. You go 'head. I'll be along in a minute.

EDDIE: I don't mind waitin' for you.

SERA: Ain't no more time for waitin'. Ain't nothin' left worth waitin' for.

EDDIE: What you mean, Sera?

SERA: Nothin', Eddie. I don't mean nothin'. You go on, now. I'll be along.

EDDIE: You sure you alright?

SERA: Yeah.

(EDDIE *begins walking off. The manner of his walk expresses his reluctance to leave. He has something to say, but can't quite muster the will or the words to do it with. He turns back to* SERA.)

EDDIE: Sera?

SERA: What is it, Eddie?

EDDIE: We've known each other a long time.

SERA: Twenty-five years.

EDDIE: Has it been that long?

SERA: You don't know?

EDDIE: My memory ain't so good no more, Sera. All I remember is the diner being almost all the time full, takin' up so much of my life there weren't no time for nothin' else.

SERA: That's how it was.

EDDIE: And you.

SERA: What about me?

EDDIE: I remember you was all the time there.

SERA: The money was good.

EDDIE: Wasn't just the money—was it?

SERA: —No.

EDDIE: —Sera?

SERA: What?

EDDIE: You was all the time there, but I couldn't see you for the diner always bein' in the way.

SERA: I guess that's right.

EDDIE: No, it ain't. It's a lie. A goddamn coward's lie. I saw you, Sera. I saw you the moment you first walked in lookin' for a job. I saw you with a feelin' I was afraid of. God Almighty, Sera, I ain't never stopped seein' you and I ain't never stopped bein' afraid. —I—damn it, Sera, I can't talk right. I never could.

SERA: This is the first time I ever heard you try.

EDDIE: Sera?

SERA: I'm listenin', Eddie.

EDDIE: Damn it, don't you know what I'm tryin' to say?

SERA: If it was 25 years ago, or 10. If it was just yesterday I'd know, but today I don't. Today I don't know nothin' so if you got somethin' to say to me you better say it.

EDDIE: *(Goes and stands near SERA.)* Do you think I oughta kneel?

SERA: Kneel? What you fixin' to do, Eddie, pray?

EDDIE: No, I ain't fixin' to pray, damn it!

SERA: Then what are you fixin' to do?

EDDIE: I'm tryin' to say somethin' to you, Sera, and you ain't makin' it any easier.

SERA: Why don't you write it down on a piece of paper and I'll say it for you.

EDDIE: Would you?

SERA: No, I wouldn't!

EDDIE: Sera, there ain't no reason to get mad.

SERA: Oh, yes there is, Eddie! A man followed me home last night and now you suddenly got somethin' to say 'sides "Sera, do this" and "Sera, do that".

EDDIE: I always said please, didn't I?

SERA: Please don't mean shit!

EDDIE: Sera!

SERA: Sera, nothin'! Lottsa times I coulda took me somebody home or gone off with 'em but I didn't, did I?

EDDIE: No.

SERA: And you know why I didn't?

EDDIE: Cuz—

SERA: Cuz I'm a goddamn fool, that's why!

EDDIE: No, it's because you a good woman.

SERA: Good? Good for what? Bein' your slave while she's your wife?

EDDIE: Who's my wife?

SERA: That goddamn Diner!

EDDIE: Sera?

SERA: Livin' with her in the day and sleepin' with her at night and all I am is a maid that comes in and cleans up.

EDDIE: I'm gonna sell the place, Sera.

SERA: A maid and a slave and that's all I am. Hired help to be told what to do. Sera do this and Sera do that and—What did you say?

EDDIE: Man been comin' 'round steady offerin' to buy the place.

SERA: Don't he know how business is?

EDDIE: He's fixin' to tear the diner down. He just wants the land it's on.

SERA: And you really gonna sell it?

EDDIE: Made up my mind this mornin'.

SERA: Awh, Eddie, you can't. It be like sellin' a part of yourself.

EDDIE: It's a part I don't mind losin' if I can have you in its place. That's what I come 'round for this mornin'. That's what I been tryin' to say. —Sera, I want you to be my wife.

SERA: Awh, Eddie.

EDDIE: I love you, Sera. I've always loved you.

SERA: Eddie, why didn't you never say nothin'?

EDDIE: The words were always there, but I wouldn't let 'em out. Sometimes they'd almost choke me wantin' to be said, but I wouldn't let 'em out. I never thought it right for me to mean anythin' to you, Sera. I never thought myself good enough. I always figured someone would come along and take you with him. I'd be sad for missin' you, but happy for knowin' you were with somebody you loved. Then last night when I seen that man follow in' after you the thought of losin' you was more than I could bear. It come to me how much you mean to me. More than that diner. More than anythin' in the world, Sera. —I know you couldn't never love nobody like me—

SERA: But I do.

EDDIE: What did you say, Sera?

SERA: I do love you.

EDDIE: Awh, Sera, you not just sayin' that, are you? I mean, you not just bein' kind, are you?

SERA: I love you, Eddie.

EDDIE: And you'll marry me?

SERA: *(Laughs warmly.)* If you're willin' to spend the rest of your days puttin' up with a gimp legged old woman, I figure I can put up with a tight lipped old geezer.

EDDIE: Oh, Sera, Sera—

SERA: What is it, Eddie.

EDDIE: *(Rushes up to SERA and grabs her hand.)* Sera, can I, uh—what I mean is could I, uh—

SERA: Jesus, Eddie, what are you tryin' to do? Break my fingers?

EDDIE: Oh, Sera, I'm sorry. I didn't hurt you none, did I? I didn't mean to—

SERA: Just be more gentle, that's all. Now gimme your hand. *(He does.)* There, that's better. What you gotta keep in mind, Eddie, is a woman's hand ain't no pot handle.

EDDIE: I'm sorry, Sera.

ACT TWO SOME RAIN 45

SERA: That's alright.

EDDIE: Sera?

SERA: What is it?

EDDIE: Sera, can I, uh—would you mind terribly much if I, uh—what I mean is, could I, uh—

SERA: For God's sakes, Eddie, say what you wanna say!

EDDIE: Can I—kiss ya?

(SERA *gets up and grabs* EDDIE *and puts a lip lock on him that takes his breath away. When it's over with* EDDIE *is weak kneed and gasping for breath.* SERA *helps him to the steps where they both sit.*)

EDDIE: Lordy, Sera, I seen it a number of times on TV, but I had no idea it was as powerful as that.

SERA: Well, if it comes as all that much of a shock to you, I better save the rest of it till after we married. I want you standin' at that altar, not lyin' down on a stretcher.

EDDIE: *(Grabs* SERA *strongly.)* By God, I'm gonna do it right now!

SERA: Do what?

EDDIE: *(Jumps up.)* Talk to the preacher! *(Begins walking off.)* There's been too much time wasted already.

SERA: Eddie, wait a minute!

EDDIE: What is it, Sera?

SERA: Come on back and sit down for a minute, will ya? I need some time to get used to this.

EDDIE: *(Returning.)* Sure, Sera.

SERA: I swear my head is spinnin' like a top. After all these years of waitin' it seems so all of a sudden.

EDDIE: Awh Sera, I can't bring back all the years lost, but we got today and every day to come for as long as God give us breath to breathe. (SERA *turns away from* EDDIE *crying.*) Sera? You cryin', Sera?

SERA: No.

EDDIE: Course you are. Now, tell me what's the matter.

SERA: It ain't nothin'.

EDDIE: It is, too. Now tell me.

SERA: *(Crying.)* I just wish you hadn't waited till I was old and ugly!

EDDIE: (EDDIE *puts his arm around* SERA *and hugs her to him.*) Sera, you always be beautiful to me and that's God's truth. (SERA *puts her head on* EDDIE'S *shoulder. A moment and* EDDIE *catches sight of something in the garden.*) Sera?

SERA: What, Eddie?

EDDIE: Your garden is sproutin'.

SERA: That can't be.

EDDIE: Well, it is. Look for yourself.

SERA: (SERA *goes to the garden and kneels.*) Oh, Eddie, them the seeds I planted so long ago I almost give up on 'em.

EDDIE: What's that one in the back different from the rest?

SERA: Where?

EDDIE: There.

SERA: Shit!

EDDIE: What is it, Sera?

SERA: A goddamn sticka bush!

(Abrupt darkness.)

THE END

PROPERTY PLOT

Act 1, scene 1

Yard:

Weeds
Rusted tin cans
Scraps of wood
Treadless tire
Rusted pipes
Paint cans
Two (2) small barrels of rusted nails
Oil barrel
Suitcase
Lock and key

Act 1, scene 2:

Yard:

All of the above

in addition:

Broom
Serving tray
Pitcher of iced lemonade
Two glasses

Act II, scene 1:

Yard and yard property same as in Act 1, scene 2, but in darkness.

Trailer:

Refrigerator
Stove
Sink
Bed
Table
Chairs
Small fan
Glasses
Plates on which are the remains of a meal
Bottle of whiskey
Suitcase
Straw hat

Act II, scene 2

Yard and yard property same as in Act 1, scene 2.

Trailer:

Refrigerator
Stove
Sink
Bed
Table
Chairs
Small fan
Glasses
Empty bottle of whiskey
Straw hat

COSTUME PLOT

Act 1, scene 1:

SERA

Hair pins
Waitress uniform
Apron
Stockings
Garters
White work shoes

WALLY

T-shirt
Dungarees
Leather work shoes (old, unpolished, scuffed)
Checkered handkerchief

Act 1, scene 2:

SERA

House dress
Slippers

WALLY

Same as Act 1, scene 1

Act II, scene 1:

SERA

Same as Act 1, scene 2

WALLY

Dress or fancy shirt (though faded and frayed, still loudly colorful)
Dungarees
Leather shoes

Act II, scene 2:

SERA

Nightgown
Slippers

EDDIE

Hat
White shirt
Suspenders
Khaki pants
White socks
Brown shoes
White handkerchief

www.ingramcontent.com/pod-product-compliance
Lightning Source LLC
Chambersburg PA
CBHW071759040426

42446CB00012B/2633